PROMISE

OF A

NEW MILLENNIUM

Published by Write Together™ Publishing LLC.
www.writetogether.com

ISBN 1-930142-52-8

Title: Promise of a New Millennium: A Time Capsule by Students of the Rutherford County Tennessee School System. Subject: 21st Century literary collections; young American authors. (Multiple authors).

Project Sponsor: Rutherford County Tennessee Board of Education,
J. Hulon Watson, Superintendent

Project Coordinators:
Laura Harper, Assistant Superintendent of Curriculum & Instruction
Elizabeth Church, Language Arts Instructional Specialist

Project Design: Jackie Drake, Administrative Assistant

Editors:
Shelia Bratton, Coordinator of Middle Level Instruction
Wendi Watts, School and Community Liaison

Publishing Advisor: Paul Clere

Cover Art: Lacy Evans, Riverdale High School, Grade 12

Typesetting & Book Design: Charles King

Promise

of a

New Millennium

A Time Capsule

by Students of the Rutherford

County Tennessee School System

Write Together™ Publishing

Nashville, Tennessee

Millennium

A now often-used word

Consisting of ten letters

That brings to mind visions

Of the past and dreams for the future.

Kelly Colvert — Oakland High School, Grade 9

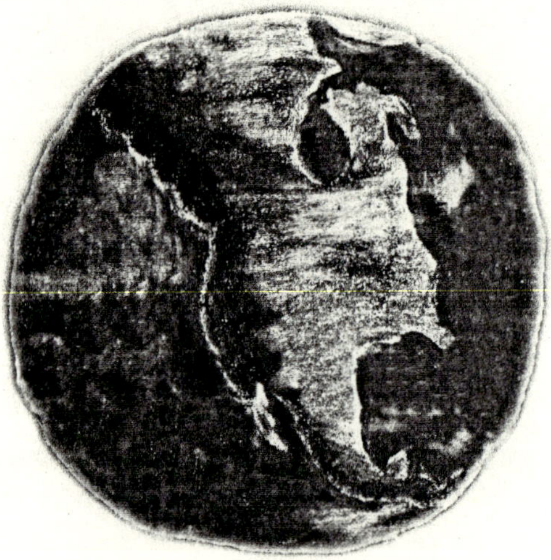

RUTHERFORD COUNTY BOARD OF EDUCATION

2240 Southpark Boulevard
Murfreesboro, Tennessee 37128
Phone (615) 893-5812 Fax (615) 898-7940

April 11, 2000

Dear Students of Rutherford County:

Thank you for sharing your letters, poems and essays in the publication *Promise of a New Millennium.* I have worked closely with young people for forty years as a teacher, coach and administrator and know that when faced with problems from their school, community or nation, students are capable of making good decisions.

When businesses, civic organizations, educational and govern-mental leaders, and students work together, problems are identified and solutions are created. The success of Rutherford County Schools is realized through the combined efforts of the total community. Our government officials and educational leaders have created a partnership that has been successful in providing our students with a well-rounded education.

As I work with the students and community leaders of today, I look forward to your *Promise of a New Millennium* with confidence that we will continue to enjoy the prosperity that we have created together.

Sincerely,

J. Hulon Watson

J. Hulon Watson
Superintendent of Schools

A Commitment to Excellence

DEAREST GRANDDAUGHTER,

AS I LOOK THROUGH MY WINDOW
I SEE MY DAYS ENDING
AS YOURS ARE JUST BEGINNING.

AMY AMONETT — CENTRAL MIDDLE SCHOOL, GRADE 8

Contributors

INTRODUCTION

The Promise of the New Millennium

Rachael South — Oakland High School, Grade 9

Promise. This word has so many meanings to it. Broken promises, secret promises, sacred promises, promises made in a heapful of laughter or tears, promises that are engraved in people's minds and hearts forever. This is what many people think of when they hear that word. Most people don't think of the real meaning of promise.

When I think of promise, I am reminded of a newlywed couple walking into an empty house. As they enter the house, they are overwhelmed with new opportunities and the feeling that they can make anything happen. They can fill the house with warm memories and happy times, or leave the home cold and empty. Promise is this feeling of overwhelming opportunity, the feeling that we can make anything happen.

Our society is like this newlywed couple. We are entering into our house, the new millennium. We have the chance to improve our environment and make our world a safer, better place in which to live, or we can just sit back and watch our world and society deteriorate. We are the only people who can make this choice. This is the promise of the new millennium.

TAKE CARE OF THE EARTH AND DON'T LET LIFE SLIP THROUGH YOUR FINGERS.

KELSEY STROOP — HOMER PITTARD CAMPUS SCHOOL, GRADE 6

The Promise of New Millennium

Jessy Brosher — Smyrna High School, Grade 11

Dear Babies, April 21, 2063

This evening after everyone had left, I sat out on the porch and thought, "Wow, eighty years." It seems like only yesterday that I was twenty-five and watching my babies, your parents, play in their sandbox. Today, instead, I watched you watching your babies, my *great*-grandbabies. As I looked upon the happy interaction of four generations, the mind-bending pace at which things have changed struck me. I remember when we ran our cars on gasoline, and we did not choose our children's characteristics from a catalog. I remember when people looked on desperately, helplessly as their loved ones fell to cancer and AIDS. I thought yet again, still rather gratefully, that sixty years ago the surgery that gave our little Karen back the ability to walk did not exist. Paralysis then was devastatingly permanent.

As I reflected on the technological advancements that have occurred within my eighty years, I couldn't help being saddened by the realization that the improvement of technology has accompanied the gradual debilitation of the close family unit. I can only believe that by the time that you all reach eighty years, family values will once again be important, and society will be less concerned with political correctness and more concerned with the instillment of a strong moral conscience. With everything our world has to offer we must remember that family is the basis of all, and life is best spent living rather than working for a bigger house or better car. If you all can remember just these few words of wisdom, then maybe you will realize, as I have, the potential that each day holds.

With all my love,
Nanna

Let not the homeless be needful of money
  to be rich in your eyes,
Nor believe the disabled to be unblessed,
Do not lose every newborn's goal of life
  by being blinded by jobs, treasures, or
  country,
For you will find the forming of age begins
  while seconds pull on skin and hours
  weaken bones,
Do not ever, my sweet child, let memories
  cover your dreams...

Matt Clark — LaVergne High School, Grade 11

An Editorial for the Millennium

Felisha Riggs — Oakland High School, Grade 9

At the dawn of a new millennium, the human race is flourishing. The economy is booming, and rates are rising. We come knocking at the door of the year two thousand with technology that our ancestors only dreamt about. Minutes, weeks, years pass before our eyes, and we barely notice. In such a fast-paced world, we must take a minute to stop and consider where we are going.

Our civilization is balanced on a fulcrum; one step either way, and we will go tumbling towards our chosen path. We choose the way we fall. Our actions now determine the future and our posterity. Though technology is proven helpful in more ways then one, it cannot win all battles. How can we rely on a man-made object to fix our man-made problems?

Change is a slow, hard-won race. Our incentive for change is simple; with each action taken, we are creating a world for the future. The world we create is our own choice. What will the year two thousand turn out to mean? Two thousand years joined together? Two thousand more children starving and homeless? Our lives are busy, yes, but each of us has the same time and obligation to stop and decide what path we will walk.

The Promise of a New Millennium
Megan Jayne — Smyrna Middle School, Grade 8

206 Milky Way
Mars, Outerspace 37167

My Dearest Grandchildren, April 5, 2067

As you very well know, I am getting to be a pretty old woman. In the eighty years I have lived on this earth, many important contributions to mankind have been made. My generation has been faced with many challenges to overcome and has had many concerns. We have overcome many of these obstacles and gone on to succeed and have many accomplishments. I think now is a good time for me to share with you the promise of a new millennium.

The year is now 2067. When I was thirteen years old, the new millennium was approaching. It was an exciting time for the whole world. However, many people were nervous and scared of a computer bug known as the Y2K bug. It was thought that all the computer systems in the world would crash when the clock switched over to 2000. It seems so silly to look back and think this was a concern to people, but during this time many people thought a computer crash would cause much confusion and turmoil.

The new millennium brought many challenges and hurdles for man to overcome. Technology had grown so much due to computers, the Internet, and other scientific research. What had only once been dreamed about was brought to life during my time. One challenge that man faced was to develop a place where man could live on Mars. Many astronauts and scientists worked hard to research the conditions on Mars and tried to find out if man could adapt to the conditions there. Scientists also worked on building cars and vehicles for man to travel in that would require less power and use resources that would never expire. Meanwhile, doctors researched many types of cancers and diseases, searching for a cure to save the lives of so many people worldwide. Man had to face these and many other challenges.

My generation accomplished so much in order to improve the standards that man lives by today. These accomplishments include the Internet, by which man can talk to people all around the world with just the click of a mouse. We also established many wildlife and other organizations that helped mankind realize how precious and valuable the earth and its resources are. We have also established more peace around the world, and made strides toward a more global democracy. Many advancements in medicine have been made, and there are now more treatments and cures for the sick than ever before. I'm very proud of the way my generation accomplished so many things that now provide your generation with the knowledge and the courage to carry on.

I hope that you have learned something about perseverance and success from this letter. Success does not come easy. It takes much hard work and determination to get to where you want to be. There is always the promise of a new day, and the chance to do something that will change the world. The promise of a new millennium is always alive. It is the knocking of opportunity at the door. Always remember that "what seems like only a ripple today, can become the wave of the future."

Love always,
xoxo Grandma

I'm eighty years old
And I'm all in the cold.
The stars are shining,
And I'm still dying
The 21st century is hard
Especially if you are poor.
Kids make fun of you
Because you shop at the Dollar General
Store.
It's not your fault
It's the adults'.

Ashley Lorenzini — Thurman Francis School, Grade 6

Chimes of Life

Amy Michaelson — Smyrna High School, Grade 11

I remember being as young as you,
And the gray Nintendos were ever-so-new,
And dolls were the "coolest" if they could talk
Compared to yours that read, write, and walk.

Life flies away faster with each living day
Tugging at your patience and causing you dismay.
With all that is changing and all that is new,
Just remember the values most important to you.

The family that has always guided you through,
The morals they have instilled in you,
The friends you'll make and the times you'll share,
And the small things in life that show people care.

As your elder and shiner of light,
From this lesson, I hope that you might
Never lose sight of the place you are going
And remember God knows the seeds you are sowing.

Sweet Child, in your future, will come forth a day
When you might need this message that I convey.
Small issues matter not when the bell of life chimes,
Only the "big-picture" issues discussed in these rhymes.

In times such as these, in a country this free,
At your door every day knocks Opportunity.
Prepare your mind, and wait with Patience
For your calling as a leader of the Next Generation.

The Story of a Lifetime

Jinan Hassan — Roy Waldron School, Grade 7

Jess, go hop in bed
Time to go to sleep
Turn the lights out
I don't wanna hear a peep.

Tell me a bedtime story
Oh Grandpa, please
He looked at her, found a chair
And settled with ease.

Okay, a long time ago
When I was just a kid
There were many problems
With the bad stuff people did.

The streets weren't safe
There were strangers with a knife
There were many dangerous people
Who tried to bring about strife.

Nothing seemed safe
Not even at school
Because of the students
Who brought guns trying to be cool.

All this new technology
And all these things we had
They made our life easier with problems
So were they really good or bad?

We had these new appliances
These new computers and DVD's
They made our life simpler
And made work a breeze.

Our world is getting better
It's not near as bad
But there's still no excuse
For the problems that we've had.

I've told you this little story
To tell you the truth
Life wasn't always easy
So enjoy it in your youth.

The new Millennium,
Is a promise that we give
It helps us be better people
And teaches us how to live.

We fought against cuts in education;
we gathered food for families in
desperation.
Battles were not the objects of our war
tales.

Becky Sullivan — Smyrna High School, Grade 11

John Wayne once said, "Life is tough, It's tougher if you're stupid!" Remember the great tragedies, for if humans don't, they are bound to repeat them.

Marshall Ziemanski — Oakland High School, Grade 10

The Promise of the New Millennium

John Bailey — Thurman Francis School, Grade 6

When I was in my younger years I accomplished many goals and made them successful. My grandson, I hope that you accomplish more than I ever did. The greatest challenge I ever had was facing my fears; I hope you will be ready for what you will experience in the generation to come. I hope that you will take your responsibilities and use your knowledge to get an education so you can get a job.

The thing that is important is to stay healthy and reach your goals. Be prepared for unexpected occasions. My concern is that you live your life the way you want in the right ways. Remember, accomplishing your goals and facing your fears and challenges will be the objectives of your childhood and your adult lifestyle.

The Millennium

Greg Jennings — Oakland High School, Grade 9

From shades of old gray
Now to a brighter light
From the alley of beggars
Comes a lighter sky
From wooden twigs
Come mallets of steel

Yesterday dissolves into tomorrow.

The Promise of a New Millennium
Becky Sullivan — Smyrna High School, Grade 11

The concerns of this generation were vast,
wondering how long our security would last.
What if this school, these halls, are next?
These are problems not covered in the text.
Will we be able to react if violence happens fast?
(funny how we think too long)

We move through the halls as if asleep
and contemplate the secrets we keep.
The new temptations are harder to face
and their effects are harder to erase.
We wonder what consequences we may reap...
(funny how the motives are wrong)

We feel inadequate next to our peers
we learn humiliation through their jeers.
Some learn patience and seek truer friends.
Some learn hate and seek harsher ends.
We're so scared of the meaning behind the leers.
(funny how the safety is gone)

What is the odd bulk in that backpack?
What if they plan on getting back?
The administrators assure our protection...
but what if someone passes their detection?
Who knows who's soon likely to crack?
(funny how the mind reels on)

Students then seek to help each other.
"Let's be open with one another."
Maybe all they need is someone to care,
maybe just help with the burdens they bear.
How easy it becomes to play the caring mother.
(funny how easy to form a bond)

We learned to stand and brave challenges well,
our hearts firm when our faces were pale.
We fought against cuts in education;
we gathered food for families in desperation.
Battles were not the objects of our war tales.
(funny how the will stays strong)

We argued with the times before,
about the wrongs of the prejudice lore.
We learned to ignore the color of a face,
and began to think of all men as one race.
We're all alike inside the core.
(funny how it took so long)

We learned that money didn't equal success,
and that power was not defined in your address.
We competed for high rank and grade,
intellect, unlike wealth, doesn't fade.
The drop-out rate became less and less.
(funny how the mind moves on)

We may not have ensured world peace,
but we learned how to be diplomatic, at least.
The world began cooling in matters of strife,
working on the *prima* cause to unify life.
Maybe in your generation the wars will cease.
(funny how time moves along)

We hated the title generation "X" at first,
and wondered why our sins were considered the worst.
But as we grew and tended our accomplishment seeds,
we realized a name would reduce our deeds.
Standing proud, we're an "X"—a variable—a first.
(funny how the heart holds on)

We must all work together to make our country a better place. I believe if everyone puts forth the effort, we can achieve our goal.

Jeff Vick — Thurman Francis School, Grade 6

...maybe we have our heads so high in the clouds that we forget to stay grounded.

Julie Price — Smyrna High School, Grade 11

The Promise of the New Millennium
Nikkia Bullard — Central Middle School, Grade 7

Things have changed from what I know
Time has passed,
And new things then have now become old.
The sun shines anew in the big blue sky
And as the world turns, so do you and I.
We age every second, every minute, every day
And these things to you are what I must say:
It is the beginning of an era, a millennium, a century
Everything seems so new, shiny, and bright
But the world often lies in its own little way,
It uses and abuses someone new every day.
So be careful what you do, and be careful what you say,
Because life almost got me that exact same way.
In closing, these words I shall leave with you today:
Follow your heart,
To thine own self be true,
Watch out for life or it will deceive you too.

To My Grandchildren
Lindsay Roe — LaVergne High School, Grade 9

To My Grandchildren,

This may surprise you, but I have learned a few things in my eighty years. I've decided to share a few of my best discoveries with you. They have made my life easier and happier and I hope that they do the same for you. The world has changed, but I believe that these secrets will hold true for many generations to come.

Get excited over the little things or you won't get excited at all. Big things to get excited over don't come along very often, but if you find something to fulfill you every day, I guarantee that your life will be full of happiness.

Never lose your imagination. Imagination seeds dreams and dreams turn into goals, and pretty soon, something you only imagined becomes a reality.

If you think things are impossible, eventually nothing will be possible. Once you begin blocking yourself from challenges to avoid disappointment you will keep doing it until you think your life is one big disappointment.

Change is inevitable. Learn to live with it, or even like it. So much change has taken place in my life. Things will keep changing as long as there are people around to change things. If you dread change you will have a whole lot to be afraid of. Change takes place every time the sun rises.

Use your knowledge to your advantage. Having these tips can change the way you think if you let them. I hope you use these and live happily ever after.

Love,
Grandmother Lindsay

The Promise of A New Millennium

Kyle Knox — Central Middle School, Grade 7

A long, long time ago,
Back in twenty-three,
People were a lot nicer and polite as they could be.

My neighbors used to be really nice,
But now they're just plain mean.
You never had to "hold a sec"
Or talk to an answering machine.

There used to be a young man,
Who would walk me across the street,
But now he's off selling drugs,
Just to keep the shoes on his feet.

I've really got my hopes up,
That someone will listen to me,
And in the millennium go back to the way,
It was in twenty-three.

Sometimes, we spend too much time looking over our shoulders, and we miss the magnificence of the road up ahead.

Marcus Patrick Ellsworth

— Oakland High School, Grade 11

I've seen a new century and an old one. I've seen people change for good and bad. My child, choose the good things. Keep God as your main focus and press on, never turning back. You will be rewarded. Do your best to better this nation, and make an even better generation than we could ever dream!

Katie Cantrell — Smyrna Middle School, Grade 8

Millennial Nightmare

Robin Bombardi — Oakland High School, Grade 9

Sometime this next millennium
    Chances are,
An asteroid will visit us—
    From afar.

And when it does, the earth will puke
    Up lava
And flaming ash, like bursting pots
    Of java.

Our roads and bridges will collapse,
    Under us,
We never thought Ma Nature would
    Rebuke us...

    For our hubris,
And give our gardens, gowns, coaches,
    To a new millennium of roaches.

The Promise of A New Generation
Nichole Napper — Roy Waldron School, Grade 7

Today I bring my final tale.
I'm getting old and my days are few
So I'll tell you a story that's from the heart;
One that includes geniuses with courage true.

"It's the end of the world!"
They shouted in predicament
As the Millennium approached us
And many lost their wit.

Of course you know by now
In the end we made it through,
As we had many other changes
Adventures and wars included, too.

As we entered the new Millennium
New peace treaties were made
And death in battle fields stopped
As our wars began to fade.

Stress faded as love flourished,
And people stopped living in vain.
And we all started to realize
That there was more to life than pain.

People started working together
To create a stronger nation.
And as people got off the streets
We put an end to all starvation.

We stopped all pollution,
And our Earth we began to cherish.
We stopped most hatred
And crime began to perish.

Our medical technology advanced,
And we learned the cure for AIDS.
Our life expectancy became higher,
And there were no more wars or crusades.

Our Army's only purpose was natural disasters,
And there were no more disturbances for us to fear,
Our National Guard was for assurance
And heartbreak was the only cause for a tear.

The new Millennium brought many promises
That made our Earth a better place
So the next generation could enjoy it
And everyone could live in a happy embrace.

Millennium
Joshua Bradford
Thurman Francis School, Grade 6

My grandchildren, whom I love,
I need to tell you about life.
Lots of things happen.
Live, love, and be kind. That's what I learned.
Earn, don't get things handed to you.
Now, you respect people, and you will get respect back.
Never hate!!!
In the future you will learn.
Until we meet again do and learn these things.
Make goals and try to meet them.

JUST REMEMBER, WHEN THE EARTH, OUR HOME,
IS CLEAN AND BRIGHT, SO ARE OUR THOUGHTS.
WHEN WE THINK CLEARLY, AND ACT ON IT, WE LOOK
ON TO A BRIGHT TOMORROW.

MEGAN LICHTWARDT — OAKLAND HIGH SCHOOL, GRADE 10

WHEN I LOOK THOUGH MY GRANDMOTHER'S EYES,
EVERYTHING IS NEW.

SHANNA BITTNER — CENTRAL MIDDLE SCHOOL, GRADE 7

Changes

Joe Zeltner — LaVergne High School, Grade 9

Why does this world often change?
Why can't everything just stay the same?
Why do kids color their hair?
Why do people often like to stare?
When I was young,
Things like that just weren't done.
Why have you all lost respect?
What else should I expect?
You kids just don't appreciate me.
Yet I still know how much you love me.
The times have changed,
Oh yes it's true.
No matter what... I still love you.

Grandchild

Michelle Leth — Central Middle School, Grade 8

My grandchild,
    how the world has grown,
and all the wonderful things,
    the world has not yet known.
Your whole life,
    is ahead of you,
but my life,
    is nearly through.
I'll leave for you,
    a few words of advice,
so you won't,
    have to walk on thin ice.
A dream,
    is always worth dreaming,
or there would be no use,
    for even breathing.
A dream,
    gives you something new,
and when you've accomplished it,
    you'll need another one, all brand new.
You shouldn't care,
    what other people think,
because all that matters,
    are the things they speak.
Don't listen to the harsh words,
    but remember the ones that matter,
and don't listen to the words,
    of unkind people as they chatter.
You'll always need,
    good friends,
that will be with you,
    to the end.

Family,
    should come first of all,
you shouldn't spend your life,
    waiting for "the" call.
Make sure,
    you choose the right one,
so your life,
    will be more fun.
The birth of your first child,
    is as important as the last,
and the now,
    is more important than the past.
Look forward,
    to everyday,
and once,
    just stop to play.
Well time is running low,
    and time is something you don't want to waste,
but don't you dare,
    set your life at a fast pace.
Now is the time,
    to say good-bye,
and when I'm gone,
    try not to cry.

Don't waste your life on only one goal. Have many. If you work hard and follow the rules, you will have no problems. Always be polite. Never be rude. Always wash your hands. So just do your best; put forth a great effort. Always respect others.

Adam Dedmon — Thurman Francis School, Grade 6

Why, oh why, are we so inconsiderate

to God's extravagant creation?

Bryan Thomas — Smyrna High School, Grade 12

Looking Over My Shoulder

Marcus Patrick Ellsworth — Oakland High School, Grade 11

The sound of small feet bounding through the hallway and two babbling voices called my attention away from the window, where I was watching the carefree flight of the butterflies flirting in the fragrant garden behind my house. As I turned around, my two grandchildren burst into the room. They looked especially innocent, so I knew they had just done something and fled the scene of the crime.

"He broke it." My granddaughter, Briana, had now taken a giant step away from her brother and was firmly pointing an accusatory finger at her doomed sibling. All my grandson, Jason, could do was stand there in a state of shock.

"But, um, see, well, I didn't break it...it...it was like that when I found it." Just when I was about to ask what exactly "It" was, Jason produced the item from behind his back. It was a small mirror shaped like an elongated four-sided diamond with elaborate crystal piping snaking its way around the edges in a beautiful tangle of light. There was also a point where the crystal formed a weighted ball so the mirror could be made to balance.

"Bring it to me." I held out my hand to take the supposedly broken object. I was more amused than I was annoyed. Jason gave me the mirror and backed away to stand next to his sister who was now smiling uncontrollably with a look of "You're gonna get it." I looked over the mirror, but I couldn't find any scratches or cracks in its silvered face.

"I don't see anything."

"Exactly, that's because he broke it." Briana said this without batting an eye. "It doesn't reflect anymore." Now I really looked into the glass. She was right. The mirror would catch the light, but wouldn't reveal even a hint of a reflection. At first I was as confused as they were, but then I remembered why it had such an odd quality. I smiled.

"All mirrors reflect something. Most of them can only show you the world around you exactly as it appears to your own eyes." Now I walked over to the coffee table and placed the object so it balanced ever so delicately on the small ball of glass at its base. "This one, however," I continued, "can only reflect the memories of whoever has owned it. In this case, it's held onto the memories that I have gathered since the dawn of the New Millennium." I placed my index fingers on the two points on its sides for a few seconds. When I removed them, it began to hum with a gently swaying sound as it spun with each rotation, getting faster than the last until the hum steadied and a faint picture could be seen in the lucid whirlwind. Briana and Jason pulled closer to the table and stared on in awe of the mirror that now revealed itself as something more but nothing less than a looking glass.

"I remember the days and hours leading up to the New Millennium." While I started my narration, the picture came into focus. The sight of huge crowds and fantastically organized celebrations faded in and out of sight. "The whole world had been holding its breath as the shadow of midnight crept around the globe, being welcomed with cheers and tolling bells. People were waiting for a revelation or a revolution, a new creation or perhaps an unforeseen destruction. None of that came as each hour's passing brought the toll of twelve and the two-thousandth year, but with each chime, change was promised."

Now, the twirling oracle showed a typical early twenty-first century city's overcrowded streets and brown air filled with the dirt and noise of a bustling populous. "Life went on as it had before, at first. Meanwhile, technological advancements were being made so quickly that the public would have new and impractical conveniences thrust upon them almost daily. While some of these advancements made life a little easier, others made it lose some of its charm and wonder." This was accompanied by pictures of people hunched over computer screens in a crowded room, where no one even looked at their neighbor while they frantically searched for a friend, even though a true one could be sitting right next to him or her.

"Science was toying with ideas about special medicines they could put in plants to help cure and prevent diseases." A scene of a Red Cross van unloading bushels of vegetables in an impoverished neighborhood was reenacted on the tiny screen. "On the other hand, controversy was being raised about cloning and whether or not it was a necessary field of research. Human cloning was banned long before it became possible and the practice itself was only limited to certain fields of research and farming." A herd of cloned sheep stampeded across the glass.

"While it seemed that the world as a whole was moving forward, the sudden occurrence of World War III brought everything to a screeching halt." The mirror seemed to turn black with the smoke and fire it portrayed. "I can still hear the sonic rifles screeching in the night like banshees calling out to the lost souls they would bring back to their dark realm. The biological weapons created during this dark age made the swift and searing light of the atomic bomb seem like a merciful weapon." Still, only fire and darkness flickered in the glass.

"After the nightmare of war was over, the world itself seemed to be in ruins. We had almost destroyed the very mother Earth from which we had sprung. As a result, a new world alliance of nations was formed. This one was stronger than any other before it, because we finally understood the fact that we needed to work together for the common goal of not only preserving ourselves, but every living thing and every gift our world has to offer." A room filled with countless leaders and translators who all seemed intent on a common, righteous goal, was seen.

"This realization led science to be geared towards harmonizing with nature instead of mimicking it or rivaling its pure beauty. The first truly electric cars were mass-produced, and service stations converted from charging by the gallon to charging by the kilowatt. Houses were built with much of the natural landscape incorporated into their structures." A small electric car buzzed into the garage of a house with lush flowering plants growing from the walls, which watered them through tiny pipes. "Eventually, all firearms were banned from domestic use, and poverty and disease are now actually being taken care of on a global scale through truly effective programs in communities that need them. For the first time in generations, people can feel safe and hopeful for the future without some dark shadow lurking over the next generation." Now the mirror showed one last reflection. This one was of my grandkids who sat across the table and stared in amazement at their own faces in the glass as it slowed down and began to wobble.

"Cool! Let me try!" Before I could stop her, Briana reached out to grab it and accidentally sent the looking glass flying to the floor where it shattered with an oddly quiet hum. She looked at me almost in tears over having actually broken the mirror.

"It's okay." I reassured her as I swept up the glass, being sure to get it all. "Sometimes, we spend too much time looking over our shoulders, and we miss the magnificence of the road up ahead." With that, I sent them outside, where they played among the carefree butterflies that had found a home in the brightly colored garden behind my house.

FOR YOUR GRANDCHILDREN YOU'LL WISH THE
SAME THING
MORE PEACE AND HAPPINESS MAY THEIR
MILLENNIUM BRING.

DAVID KING — CENTRAL MIDDLE SCHOOL, GRADE 7

The Promise of a New Millennium

Rokeita Henry — Oakland High School, Grade 10

To my young grandchildren I leave this note,
In this poem my life I quote,
Of the good, the bad, the hard, and the easy,
And how my life seems quite pleasing.
School and college helped my success
To excel in the world of business.
Though many things made me want to quit,
I'd close my eyes and prayed to get through it.
Some years later I met a man,
Who through marriage took my hand.
With my new half we made a child,
Who made our living all worth while.
Though times grew hard with verges of war and stuff,
And our income wasn't quite enough.
To make a living, I'd work real late
To put some food on our plate.
And through the years our family and income grew.
Your parents became grown and then came you.
I'd like you to know that living in the 21st century wasn't
easy;
But through it all, my life has been quite pleasing.

Y2 SCARE

Kellye Croft — Smyrna Middle School, Grade 8

It was the world's birthday, our two-thousandth year
everyone was filled with Y2K fear,
as the clock ticked closer and the day grew near
people stocked their cupboards for the New Year.
Many watched as midnight came
and everything ended up the same,
every one partied into the night
without worrying it ended to be all right.
When we all were afraid of that "Y2K Bug"
it ended up to be a "Y2K Slug."
As I look back on the memories I say,
I hope the next millennium doesn't turn out this way!

No Promises

Jon Kinney— Oakland High School, Grade 9

The new millennium,
A time of change will be.
Inventions, we will make.
Alliances, we will break
Throughout the world and sea.

But naught is guaranteed
To humans on this Earth.
For there will be to come,
Then this cursed world is done,
A day to death and rebirth.

Honesty in the Year 2000

Neely Van Dorp — Oakland High School, Grade 9

Our time is come
With morbid defiance
Children betraying the
Mistaken alliance
We're no longer inhibited
By childhood fear
This bereft generation
Will unite in our year
With silently found knowledge
And quiet lost in youth
We have lessened the
Ache of lamentable decades
And supplied our Earth
With what is always denied
Truth.

Y2K

Daniel Elrod — Oakland High School, Grade 9

"It's the end of the world," everyone said.
"When Y2K comes we'll all be dead."
They had us believing, but now we are seeing,
You can't always trust what you've read.

LIFE IS BEST SPENT LIVING RATHER THAN WORKING FOR A BIGGER HOUSE OR BETTER CAR.

JESSY BROSHER — SMYRNA HIGH SCHOOL, GRADE 11

THE BIGGEST CHALLENGE WILL BE PRESSURES. PRESSURES FOR DRUGS, TO BE COOL, TO BE MEAN, FOR EVERYTHING THERE IS PEER PRESSURE. DON'T LISTEN TO YOUR TEMPTATIONS; THEY'LL LEAD TO UNHAPPINESS.

CAITLIN ORR — THURMAN FRANCIS SCHOOL, GRADE 6

Life

Brook Williams — Riverdale High School, Grade 11

We are born together into our daily lives
To share our loves, heartbreaks, and falls.
We are brought together in our daily
Lives to spread joys, heartbreaks, and sometimes our sorrows.

We are brought together in love and marriage
By God's will and nature's way
We are given love and marriage so the love shall never die
    and
So life will be bright and beautiful

We are alone in death.
Death is nature's way of rebirth.
We share the heartbreak for the love and
Soul of the departed one.

Strangers black, white, blue, and purple
Are brought together in the afterlife
To pray to go back or
Pray to stay and celebrate something more
Than all the world can express.

Song for the Children

Sarah Grissom — LaVergne High School, Grade 9

It is a song for our generation
Full of our joys and lamentations
A song to be sung for the children.

With drumbeat fast in the fury of war
The cymbals for bombs and the peace they tore
A gong and timpani in a soft moaning sound
For the little ones whose parents lie now in the ground
Let them listen
'Tis a song for the children.

With a bow upon strings playing soft and high
For the days of joy that pass quickly by
For the grass of green
The skies of blue
The wonders of life
Clear and true
Such a beautiful melody
All for the children.

Let them hear the music
The good parts and the bad
A fanfare of trumpets for the works of man
Take our discoveries
Take them in hand
Use our technology,
Let it expand
Write new parts for the song
For your children.

Let them hear the music
The good parts and the bad
Let them see the sorrow
And the good times that we've had.
Let them hear the music
It is everywhere
The song is for the children.

Millennium?

Chris Young — Oakland High School, Grade 9

Violent political storms.
Raging overseas wars.
New problems every day.
This is our new millennium?

Racial slurs thrown about.
People's lives tossed out.
Waves of new diseases spread.
This is our new millennium?

Men without their morals.
Women without homes.
Children without food.
This is our new millennium?

OUR MAIN SCHOOL CONCERN HAS BEEN SCHOOL VIOLENCE — STUDENTS KILLING OTHER STUDENTS BECAUSE OF HATRED, JEALOUSLY, RELIGION, OR JUST TO CAUSE PROBLEMS.

RACHEL CHARLTON — SMYRNA MIDDLE SCHOOL, GRADE 8

THE BIRDS HAVE ALL STOPPED SINGING.
THE RIVERS HAVE ALL RUN DRY.
THE HEAVENS HOLD NO MYSTERY,
FOR WE HAVE HOUSES IN THE SKY.

JULIE WATSON — OAKLAND HIGH SCHOOL, GRADE 9

Directions of Life

Justin Fields — LaVergne High School, Grade 9

In the beginning
life was full of joy.
Then people began using
guns as a toy.

As a child,
carefree I was.
As a youth,
I learned the truth.

My teenage years
saw hate and crime,
but through God's help
we bide our time.

Life progressed
as God had planned,
and, in his will,
we took a stand.

Times got worse
and people lost hope.
Some even came
to the end of their rope.

Troubles came my way
but God saw me through,
and the same help he gave me,
He can give you.

The Promise of the New Millennium: The Struggle of Life
Kristi Gatlin — Smyrna Middle School, Grade 8

Life has taken me far and set me in my place,
with unexpected turns and an unpromised pace.
But it wasn't so easy to get where I am now.
It's hard to explain what I did to get here and how
Time changes a person, for both better and worse,
but it all depends on what you practice and rehearse.
Certain things will make you bolder or stronger.
They help you enjoy life and let you live longer.
The secret to getting where you want to find yourself,
is to obtain what will help you as a person,
whether it be happiness or wealth.
I chose to take each day as it came.
I filled those days with worthwhile acts and things that made
me happy and gave me fame.
Each generation finds that life is more difficult for them than
the people living in the current, but I think it is a matter
of what life has given you and what you gave in return
for it.
And now it is up to you to decide in what ways you can make
this world an ideal place to live.
You must learn to give everything that you can possibly give.
First, decide what you have to give to yourself.
Make sure you are happy with where you stand and your
health.
Then you can move on to improve all of your surroundings,
to set a place for yourself with absolutely no boundaries.
Many goals have been set in my lifetime for the future,
but the goals weren't always met by their makers; they
were met by the pursuers.
The goals reached have included better transportation,
easier ways to make money, and greater means of
communication.

But not only have they helped the material things that exist,
they have also helped make realities out of someone's
hope or their wish.
Those who lived with no homes or food to indulge,
now have a roof over their heads and tummies that bulge!
There once were people who were locked up as if in chains
and lived in a country where the leaders did not believe
in change.
But now they have freedom and happiness in their lives.
They've overcome their fears, bad days, and strifes.
Whether your goals are to help out in a large or small way,
take what comes day to day.
Do what makes you happy... don't worry about all the others,
because when jealousy comes about, it doesn't leave,
it hovers.
It doesn't matter how anyone else feels about you,
it matters what you think about your life when it is
through.
When it comes to life, stakes are set quite high.
Make sure you overcome those stakes before the day you die.
You never know when that day will arise,
it doesn't come loudly, it comes in disguise.
So, do what you must and leave something behind when
you're through,
because there are other people waiting behind you
intending to begin anew.

MAKE SURE YOU CAN GET AN EDUCATION,
BECAUSE WITHOUT AN EDUCATION
YOU CAN'T GET A GOOD JOB.
YOU NEED A GOOD JOB IN ORDER TO LIVE AND
ACCOMPLISH EVERYTHING IN YOUR LIFE
THAT YOU EVER WANTED.
YOU HAVE ONLY A LIFETIME.
DON'T EVER GIVE UP, AND DON'T EVER SAY YOU
CAN'T DO SOMETHING,
UNLESS YOU'VE TRIED.
STAY OUT OF TROUBLE,
BE GOOD,
AND STAY TRUE TO YOURSELF.

JENNA HICKERSON — SMYRNA MIDDLE SCHOOL, GRADE 8

Cloning

Anne Rucker — Oakland High School, Grade 9

A hundred years ago
You never would have seen,
A person walking down the road
With their clone following.

Well, now we're in a brand new age
With brand new things to see,
Lots of new inventions
Including, a clone of me.

She follows me from place to place
To everywhere I go,
She is my very own best friend
She's the perfect girl, I know.

It's like I have a sister
That just popped up one day,
She looks and acts just like me
In every possible way.

Sometimes it's confusing
Having two of me,
And when we take out pictures
I cannot tell between.

But some days I sit and wonder
If she knows that she's a clone
And on the day that she finds out,
Will she want one of her own?

My Gifts from the Old Millennium

David Pegel — Smyrna Middle School, Grade 8

An old laptop from the late twentieth century,
A Palm Pilot from the early twenty-first.
Priceless artifacts with little or no value
That still work, however, obsolete.
These go to you, grandchild.

An old wedding ring.
Coming from an ancient custom
Where couples gave rings when they wed
Instead of genes.
This also goes to you, grandchild.

When I look back over the years,
Memories come and manifest.
Times when we were at war
And times when we were at peace.
These stories go to you, grandchild.

Last, but far from least, my love.
And my promise that your generation
Will stretch out
And solve the problems that we sparked.
This goes to you last, grandchild.

Finally, my legends
Not given to you to keep, but to share.
There were times when our grandparents,
Whom you sadly will never know,
Gave legends to me as their grandchild.

My blessings go to you and your parents;
My wonderful son
And his beautiful wife,
With such wonderful traits
That I hope your wife will have, grandchild.

They lived in a time I am sure you have heard of,
The Latter Depression;
It was actually a Revolution
Where we learned to abandon money forever.
Money is a danger that I try to protect you from, grandchild.

Now we pass the legacy to you:
Do good things in our eyes and save others.
Remember, as long as what you do is right,
You will always be worthy
Of being my grandchild.

TROUBLES CAME MY WAY

BUT GOD SAW ME THROUGH,

AND THE SAME HELP HE GAVE ME,

HE CAN GIVE YOU.

JUSTIN FIELDS — LAVERGNE HIGH SCHOOL, GRADE 9

...BELIEVE IN YOURSELF THROUGH THE GOOD TIMES AND THE BAD TIMES. YOU CAN DO ANYTHING YOU WANT TO DO IF YOU JUST BELIEVE. AND IN ANYTHING YOU WANT TO DO, ALWAYS STRIVE FOR THE BEST.

BRANDON OLIVER — THURMAN FRANCIS SCHOOL, GRADE 6

Under an Alien Sky

Trey Amerson Pegram — Oakland High School, Grade 11

As I sit on my porch and look to the sky,
I see barren Earth and begin to cry.
What beasts, what animals that ruined our land
When hatred and the heart went hand in hand.
They fought with great malice in what came to be
The war of all wars to be designated by "III."
All hopes for survival lay within the stars.
Thus marked man's first expedition to Mars.

Forced to compromise the beliefs of all races,
Mars' new inhabitants learn to look beyond faces.
A deep love and understanding sweep the land fast,
Which was never felt by those of the past.
Words like "races" and "different" were all left behind,
And mankind looked upon others as mankind.

The Millennium

Jonathan Seymore — Oakland High School, Grade 9

The Millennium,
A thousand years
Ahead of us,
And in them,
What will come?
Will there be
A peace of nations
Or another
Multitude of wars?
What will come
Into our realm
Of practicality
And possibility?
What kind of
Technological advances
Will we make
This thousand years?
Will the
End of the world come,
Or will we see another
Millennium?
And last and
Most importantly,
What will happen
To us?
Only time
Can unveil
The secret of
Our futures.

The Promise of a New Millennium

Rachel Cheek — Smyrna High School, Grade 11

Dear My Beloved Grandchildren,

Being your grandmother, as well as your senior, I feel it is my duty to pass on to you some wisdom I have attained from the experiences of my life. The age-old art of storytelling, although entertaining, is also a superb manner of educating. I have chosen the written form of communication solely to stress the importance of my words. Now children, pay close attention to all that I have to say. I promise it will not be a drawn out tale of how I trudged three miles to school every morning in the snow when I was younger.

At the turn of the twenty-first century there was an eagerness in the air, a hunger for knowledge. This is now commonly referred to as the age of technology and discovery, the Third Great Awakening. Education was the most valuable possession a person could own. During this time the cure for AIDS and most types of cancer was found, crime rates dropped to an all-time low, and moral values reigned supreme. People came to hold the motto "Progress not Regress." They set aside their petty differences and united to produce a world free from prejudices. Not to say that the world became a utopia, but looking back on those years it is the positive occurrences that I recall as being the most influential to the future.

This era is the foundation of the world you kids live in today. It is not what happened, but more so, the mentality that was created. Humans finally learned the true meaning of respect, and willfully gave it to one another. My children, I ask you to carry this frame of mind with you as you travel to the end of this century and beyond.

Your loving Grandmother

I FEEL THAT LIFE DURING THE 21ST CENTURY WAS WONDERFUL IN MANY WAYS BECAUSE THINGS OFFERED TO A PERSON OPENED DOORS OF OPPORTUNITIES TO THEM. BUT IN CERTAIN WAYS I FEEL THAT MANY FAILURES IN THE ECONOMY PUT FLAWS IN THE 21ST CENTURY TIME PERIOD. FOR ME THOUGH, I FEEL MUCH OF THE 21ST CENTURY IS RECORDED IN EVERYONE'S LIVES BECAUSE WE ALL EXPERIENCED AT LEAST A SMALL PORTION OF IT.

SARAH VISOCKY — MCFADDEN SCHOOL, GRADE 6

Time

Josh Yohe — Smyrna Middle School, Grade 8

The inclusion of technological advances to control and
monitor this force
Has, in its conquest, destroyed those who had
Harnessed and contemplated over its welfare.
It feeds on power,
Thirsts for the hearts and souls within its path.

Eroding all that comes before it
With a merciless hunger to strive forward.
As it comes to the beginning of another year, century,
Millennium, it does not matter.
It now becomes more luminous in the universe
With the sole purpose to come forth into the hands of men,
So that they may harvest it,
Feed on its adversity.

Yet you ask me of what is to come,
And how am I to report that only one thing,
Can tell you and explain it to you,
But is invisible to the eye,
Not to the heart and soul.

The Promise of a New Millennium
Tara Barrier — Smyrna High, Grade 11

To the Children of the New World:

As I was once a young soul, I too, remember the trials brought forth to my generation. Elders looked upon us with enthusiastic, luminescent faces filled with hope that we would become the peacemakers of our ever-widening world. However, although we were quick to fill our desires to please them, we did not fully comprehend the task of caring for our new world. Our hearts were mixed with emotions of excitement and fear. It was not until much later that we would realize the naiveté of our excitement to mend the gaping sores left by years of hardship and war. With a sense of confidence and knowledge, we catapulted ourselves into the task of healing the world without ever ensuring a way out.

One of the greatest challenges left to our generation was to find cures for ever-widening diseases such as AIDS. For many years we struggled, falling and rising all in the same day. And every time we erred we somehow became stronger and more able to complete the task set before us because we had gained some knowledge of its immunity. Now, as an adult, I realize that many people believe us to be foolish because of the immense and seemingly unattainable goals we set for ourselves. Although our generation did not cure the entirety of the world's problems, we laid the beginning of the foundation for what the future may bring to science, medicine, and wisdom. It is not up to one single generation to build upon the knowledge that has been both preserved and accumulated over the years. Rather, it is through the hard work of other colleagues who share a similar belief that man is victorious in attaining any goal so long as he never believes in the word "defeat." A population will flourish and become richer in knowledge, health, and morality. No goal is impossible; reach for the stars.

Love,
A Fellow Contributor

The One, True Question

Lindsay Vaughn — Oakland High School, Grade 9

I look up at the stars, and I imagine,
A thousand years ago,
Someone just like me staring up at these brilliant diamonds
In the black void of space
And wondering what the next thousand years
Has in store for mankind.
She is plain, yet in her eyes one can see
That this question has taken over her thoughts.

Now, as I look up at these same stars,
The same question haunts me.
So much has happened in the past thousand years.
Things change, people evolve and try
To comprehend the world around them.
It seems that the only truth lies within us,
And, if we stare long enough,
We may find it in the stars.

GOD KNOWS THE SEEDS YOU ARE SOWING.

AMY MICHAELSON — SMYRNA HIGH SCHOOL, GRADE 11

NOW YOU SEE SOME GOOD AND BAD CHANGES OF THE WORLD. IT IS UP TO THE NEXT GENERATION TO PRESERVE THE GOOD CHANGES AND IMPROVE THE BAD. YOU ARE THE NEXT GENERATION, SO IT IS UP TO YOU.

AMY COFFEY — SMYRNA MIDDLE SCHOOL, GRADE 8

The Promise of a New Millennium

Quin Zlotky — Riverdale High School, Grade 9

We accomplished and achieved, my generation and I. We
followed through our plans.
Even though we fought and grieved, we finished by joining
hands.
They said we were the slackers. They called us
Generation X.
We were all the bad kids. They never knew what we would
do next.
Now I'll admit we were different, strange in our own way,
But we grew up and fulfilled our dreams with the dawn of
each new day.
We traveled space and put robots on Mars. I know to
you that's small.
We discovered new things like electric cars, but I can't name
them all.
We found and conquered, explored it all, and one day you
will see.
Someday your generation will be just as proud as me.

The Buildings Have All Changed

Julie Watson — Oakland High School, Grade 9

The buildings have all changed
And the streets are all brand new.
Things that used to bring me joy
Are now broken and misused.

The birds have all stopped singing.
The rivers have all run dry.
The heavens hold no mystery,
For we have houses in the sky.

There are computers in our kitchens
And no one working in our stores.
Our homes have security systems
We even have self-cleaning floors.

We don't have to think as much—
We have things that do that, too.
Our beaches are paved over
To make a shopping mall or two.

Well, we used to play on playgrounds
But now it's on our PCs.
We used to go to concerts
But why? It's all on DVD.

So welcome to the future—
It's a great place to be
If you like fake intelligence
And miles and miles of concrete.

Because the buildings have all changed
And the streets are all brand new
The things that used to bring me joy
Are now broken and misused.

Changes

Demetria Custer — LaVergne High School, Grade 9

In the year 2066 at the age of eighty
I'll look over my life to see how the world's
Changed me.

I'll see the new technology that the world brings
The kind that makes what we use now
Seem like antique things.

I'll write a diary of all the new things I'll see
And I'll write about stuff that's sacred to me.

I'll try to remember things from my past
The things I thought would always last.

The good memories, the bad memories, and
Even the sad,
Would remind me of the life I once had.

So in the year 2066 at the age of eighty
I'll look over my life to see how the world has
Changed me.

My promise of the New Millennium is to treat everyone fairly and not put people down, because God put us on this earth to treat people the same way we want to be treated.

Brittany Taylor — Thurman Francis School, Grade 6

Ours was an age of interminable ignorance and isolation. We struggled with technology in order to become more connected to the whole of society, but we found ourselves to be more distant than ever.

Will Pinson — Oakland High School, Grade 11

Future

Dustin Atkin — Oakland High School, Grade 9

As all of the years have gone by
 and I have grown old and weak,
So too have all grown around me
 and all is not as foreseen.

So true, all is not same,
 and all does not differ.
Yes, good times there have been
 but more frequently bad.

Unlike simple ages yester,
 all is bare and unjust.
Although unspoiled places there are,
 their number is not many.

Yielded to none it is all our own
 and yet some choose not to possess.
Once was it said we are makers of our own future,
 What shall yours be?

At the Turn of the Century

Joshua Stewart-Dortch — Smyrna High School, Grade 10

At the turn of the century,
The world wasn't all that great of a place.
There was filth on the streets,
Liars in office,
Although some good was here.
Some people were great,
Some didn't lie, some didn't cheat,
Some were wonderful until the end.
The end, ah the end.
How we all thought it was near.
We were wrong,
We see that now.
Now our streets are just filthier,
The people in office are worse.
No one believed me when I said,
This world is coming to an end.

Respect is the Key
Bryan Thomas — Smyrna High School, Grade 12

We breathe in its air, trample on its ground,
and rarely show appreciation.
Why, oh why, are we so inconsiderate
to God's extravagant creation?
During our era, we have a family,
and usually, a pretty good friend.
But what shall we do, in our time,
before it comes to an end?
We may go to college, get an office job,
or take a great vacation.
What shall the people do, however,
when we are faced with over-population?
Now, we see less snow each winter,
and the sun gets hotter and hotter.
What will the world attempt, however,
when we begin to run out of water?
We step outside to enjoy the weather,
ahhh, the gentle breeze.
But what does this wind amount to,
when we are faced with a deadly disease?
We grow inconsiderate every day,
wanting more and more.
What will it take for us to come to our senses?
Perhaps, a nuclear war?
Many causes exist that may end the world,
we must decide to make the move.
Respect for the earth is all I ask,
and gradually it will improve.

MONEY IS A DANGER THAT I TRY TO PROTECT YOU FROM, GRANDCHILD.

DAVID PEGEL — SMYRNA MIDDLE SCHOOL, GRADE 8

ONE OF THE GREATEST CHALLENGES FOR TEENAGERS, I BELIEVE, IS TO KEEP THEIR MORALS IN THIS CRAZY WORLD. I FEARED TO GO TO SCHOOL SOMETIMES; I SINCERELY HOPE THAT IT IS NOT LIKE THIS FOR YOU. I WISH YOU THE BEST OF LUCK IN LIFE AND... ENCOURAGE YOU TO DO YOUR BEST TO IMPROVE SOCIETY.

TAVIA GARLAND — OAKLAND HIGH SCHOOL, GRADE 10

The Promise of a New Millennium

Melissa Srygley — Smyrna High School, Grade 11

Hey Kiddos!

I was sitting here just thinking of my dear grandchildren while watching a documentary on "Life during the 1990's." While watching the program I couldn't help but reminisce about the days when I had been a teenager like you. I remember the developed technology I used which now seems prehistoric to you. I loved nothing more than driving home in my gas-run car, using the phone, and watching the two-dimensional television. But now we all have even more devices to make our lives easier such as cars run by means that do not pollute the atmosphere, phones that fit in our ear, and televisions that project 3-D images.

I remember the society being filled with health, business, and technology concerns far more critical than the concerns today. With the development of medicines to cure cancer and other fatal diseases, the world has become a safer and healthier place to live. The business and political worlds have made huge advancements for the economy. With no national debt and the rapidly decreasing percentage of poverty, the United States has definitely made a huge financial change for the better.

The now non-existent issue of racism was a problem during the years I was a teen. The thought of no war and no racial discrimination seemed unreal back then. It has been amazing to stand back and watch throughout the years how the world has come together, undivided by ethnic boundaries.

I hope this letter helps you appreciate the conveniences and better conditions existing in the world today. Though I remember loving life in the 1990's the future always brings hope.

Love Always,
Nanny

To Whom It May Concern
Julie Price — Smyrna High School, Grade 11

To Whom It May Concern:

As I look back at my life, I am amazed how the world has "improved." Sure, technology has increased in power, but has this power gained by technology affected the power individuals possess? Are flying cars really necessary? Sometimes I think that maybe we have our heads so high in the clouds that we forget to stay grounded. I am not unhappy with the progress of the past few generations, but I am not without concern for our future.

I plan to live another thirty years without question. If I'm lucky, I'll live longer —fifteen, twenty more years maybe? The expansions in the medical field have exceeded what I had envisioned of them — they're surreal, as far as I'm concerned. "Incurable" diseases are at an all-time minimum; of course, after micro-technologists cured cancer and AIDS, the other diseases soon disappeared. People live well into their second century with ease. My distress is of the condescending attitude that society has towards life. Those simple necessities have been taken for granted: automatic fueling (for cars), light cookers (microwaves but faster), the sun... When was the last time you took a deep breath and realized how lucky you are to be alive? Besides, the increase of technology brought problems. Why do we have a 105 miles per hour speed limit? My mother was outraged by the change from 60 to 70 miles per hour! Although cars are safer now, accidents are more frequent. Vaccinations from viruses are proving ineffective lately, also. Viruses and bacteria have grown stronger and stronger over the years. I dread the next flu season.

As for discoveries, scientists have made quite a few. Astronomers and physicists have found the mass of gravity, and also, discovered that wormholes *do* exist. Amazingly enough, we never made a colony on Mars or the moon. We did visit Mars and Jupiter and Saturn, but the studied areas weren't acceptable for living. The Mir space program has become a small city now — the easiest way to slow down the world's population. I continue to be in awe of the magnificent people who make these discoveries.

Since the turn of the century, physical wars have ceased. Verbal and economic arguments have been the extent of war. However, no war does not mean no problems. Revolts and riots over governmental and social power continue without progress.

I wish for future generations that they overcome the power of technology and learn to handle it more effectively, live peacefully, and, individually, find the inner joy that cannot be stifled once it appears. These challenges are not easy to conquer, but with the knowledge and passion of modern man, they should be attainable.

My Grandmother's Eyes

Shanna Bittner — Central Middle School, Grade 7

When I look though my grandmother's eyes,
Everything is new.
All these things are happening;
They all came out of the blue.
All of a sudden there is the Internet, CDs, and so much more,
Plus, advanced technology galore.
She can remember when things were simple and plain.
Now people are held in chains,
They are put in jail for crimes committed—
I cannot imagine how it must feel
To witness all this change, joy, and distress,
Now the world is such a mess.

A DREAM,

IS ALWAYS WORTH DREAMING,

OR THERE WOULD BE NO USE,

FOR EVEN BREATHING.

MICHELLE LETH — CENTRAL MIDDLE SCHOOL, GRADE 8

IF YOU TRY YOUR BEST IN LIFE, YOU WILL ACHIEVE YOUR GOALS.

AMANDA LAMB — THURMAN FRANCIS SCHOOL, GRADE 6

I Look Towards the Future

John Garner — Oakland High School, Grade 9

I look towards the future,
Grey uncertainty obscures my view,
I catch glimpses of sights,
    Some pleasant, some disturbing,
    Miracles, atrocities, freedoms, fears— all there.

I turn away; perhaps I am afraid of what I may see,
But the curiosity burns in my soul.
Trembling, I look again,
    Collapse of governments, religious fevor, scientific
        breakthroughs,
    Moral dilemmas, war, disease control— also there…

Enough! I wish to see no more, be it good or bad,
The sword of the future has two blades,
One kind, the other malevolent,
Both good and bad are eternal, though one may be stronger
    at one time,
And if the future is evil, we will always have hope to
    strengthen us.

My Millennium

Jamie Shearer — Riverdale High School, Grade 9

Man has now walked on the moon and Mars
Traveled the earth to see the stars
Gone from horse, to car, to plane
Man on this earth has seen much change
Diseases that killed now have a cure
What life has in store no one knows for sure
The predictions we've made were not up to par
Even to this day man cannot see that far
Great minds have spoken all in their time
And found new intelligence that has left us behind
We have searched other planets for what we call life
And what has been found we have put to the knife
Violence still overcomes good
Even in my day we knew that it would
Equal rights back then is what they preached
But now they say male only knows how to teach
We've survived things big as wars even small as computer
overloads
So why do they insist this world will explode
Churches from my day stood their ground
But no one is in them, "The Word" yet not found
Overpopulation has now been put to rest
No one on this earth even cares to take a breath
All thought we would be happy to see more than just earth
Now earth is no more than an every day perch
As painful as all the words in this poem might seem
To Me this Millennium did not seem to gleam
So if there is any advice that I have to give
Live your life as it pleases you for it is the only one you have
to live.

The Promise of the New Millennium

Heather Ruse — Oakland High School, Grade 9

If a world could change,
It would be free of all its impurities,
No hate or violence,
Regardless of gender or race.

If a world could change,
The air would be fresh,
The water would be clean,
Earth would be preserved.

If a world could change,
Children would all have loving homes,
Poverty would be non-existent,
Education would be the key.

If a world could change,
Drugs would not take lives,
Cures for all diseases would be made,
Even for AIDS.

If a world could change,
Wouldn't life be perfect?
But life can never be perfect...
Because can a world really change?

You do not play as we used to play. There are not many trees left for you to climb, streams to wade through, fields to indulge your sports. Only the technology for the day, subtly forced upon you in hopes for a better society.

Sarah Sutton — Homer Pittard Campus School, Grade 6

Set an example for those around you. Make good choices. People are people, and everyone should be in someone else's life for good things.

Lindsay Oliver — Thurman Francis School, Grade 6

My Younger Life

Kevin Davis — Central Middle School, Grade 8

In the years before your time
I was a young man in my prime.
Paintball was my rage
And my field was our stage.
American Eagle was the brand.
Some of our clothes were blasted by sand.
Old Navy was the best.
Structure took up all the rest.
Going to the Y and church to see my friends.
Somehow all the fun never ends.
Some of my music, my mom hated.
She did like a lot of the girls I dated.
This is about all I have to say about the past.
Your life will run by just as fast.

The Promise of a New Millennium

Will Pinson — Oakland High School, Grade 11

Dear Grandchildren,

Ours is the world in which you live and grow, and you will live and grow to pity us. You are the uncompromising reminders of squandered opportunities and dreams deferred. Yet you are beacons to us. You are the shining light that guides us into the harbor of hope and away from the jagged coastline that is the drudgery of everyday life in the twenty-first century.

Ours was an age of interminable ignorance and isolation. We struggled with technology in order to become more connected to the whole of society, but we found ourselves to be more distant than ever. We traded the beautiful solemnity of a quiet winter morning and the gentle satisfactions of summer evenings for the cheap thrills offered by technology. We allowed the desire and hunger for life to acquiesce to the temptations of an easier existence through a modem.

Ours is the mess you see today. We torched the skies and murdered our neighbors in the names of fear and the almighty dollar. In the midst of all the destruction we forgot to preserve the most important aspect of life, life itself. We alone are dirty and stupid, covered in the soot and stench of the blood of our fellow humans. We are the guilty parties in the rape and destruction of grace, virtue, and innocence.

Ours are your parents, a generation who, like their parents, sold out and gave up. They are the pitiful masses poised to take over a mess that they are too old to escape yet too young to affect. God save them.

Yours is the future. We have made our bed and shall soon lie in it, but you are not lost. Your life will be what you make of it. The chains that our generation has forged will fade along with us. And whenever you are out on a quiet winter morning and the wind stirs up the dry snow from out of nowhere and the only sounds you hear are the sounds of your feet plodding through the drifts of God's fleeting powder, remember me and appreciate the beauty of life in the years to come. Good luck.

GET EXCITED OVER THE LITTLE THINGS OR YOU WON'T GET EXCITED AT ALL.

LINDSAY ROE — LAVERGNE HIGH SCHOOL, GRADE 9

PLEASE, CHERISH LIFE;

IT IS WAY TOO DELICATE TO LOSE.

SHANNON PITTS — THURMAN FRANCIS SCHOOL, GRADE 6

The Promise of the New Millennium

J.D. Rhodes — Central Middle School, Grade 7

Listen children of the child of mine,
And listen well to what the teller of tales wants you to find.
This message is carried on golden angel wings,
And sung by the birds of the heavenly rings.
This is a tale of a beautiful promise,
The promise of a new Millennium.
This Millennium ran on incredible power,
Time grew greater by every hour,
The mind of man was streaming with life,
And the evil inside was pierced with a silver knife.
Love was the core of every heart,
Peace was buried in one's very soul,

And victory was everyone's goal.
The sun shone brighter than it ever did before,
Destroying the shadows of hate, grief, and gore.
Smiles were upon every enlightened face,
And the power of heaven shown in almighty grace.
And the birds sang their songs as they flew quickly by,
As the clouds did their dance in the massive northern sky.
This is the promise of a millennium new,
And the question of its staying all depends on you.
This earth is a loving and beautiful sight,
But it can all be destroyed by Evil's might.
So guard it you must, children of the child of mine,
And always let earth's magnificent love be yours to find.

The Promise of a New Millennium

Crystal McKay — Thurman Francis School, Grade 6

The promise of a new millennium — what does that mean actually? Is that to say that in the years to come life's walk will be vast and unimaginably wonderful, or is it to say that whales and dolphins will just be a story that we tell to our grandchildren? Will we live in a world with smog-filled skies, or will the air be so clean and crisp that you would be able to see for miles into the heavens?

In the years to come I think the world could be a place where the streets are paved with gold. As you look outside you would be able to see all of the houses with their doors wide open enjoying the fresh air. There would be no poverty in the years to come, for everyone would be able to live in peace. The number of accidents would be cut down because of electronics in the road. Cars and buses will soar through the air like gentle flying birds in the night sky. People having fun and enjoying themselves would now become a reality. I think that in the future there will be medicines to cure cancer and AIDS. I believe that every person could have a better education and a better perspective toward life.

In the years to come I think the world could be a place were every step you take could be your last. Every time you take a breath you could be endangering yourself because of the pollution in the air which every person has helped create. I think people will concentrate more on partying and having fun than studying and getting an education. This would result in more poverty. Everyone would have his or her own cardboard box to call home, what kind of life is that?

What the world is like in the years to come is what you make it out to be.

Poem to My Grandson

Paul Morgan — Kittrell Elementary, Grade 6

This world is a hard place
I had to see it face to face...
The world's insanity can turn you around
Just the sight of it can throw you down
Just as I thought this world was fine
Earth sent shivers down my spine
I carried my entire load
Down this world's dusty road
Now I leave this world to you
In hopes that you can carry through...

ONE OF MY BIGGEST HOPES FOR YOU IS THAT YOU CAN LIVE IN A WORLD AWAY FROM VIOLENCE BECAUSE IT DOESN'T SOLVE ANYTHING.

MEGAN ROBINSON — THURMAN FRANCIS SCHOOL, GRADE 6

WILL WE LIVE IN A WORLD WITH SMOG-FILLED SKIES, OR WILL THE AIR BE SO CLEAN AND CRISP THAT YOU WOULD BE ABLE TO SEE FOR MILES INTO THE HEAVENS?

CRYSTAL MCKAY — THURMAN FRANCIS SCHOOL, GRADE 6

The Promise of the New Millennium

Carolyn Goodman — Homer Pittard Campus School, Grade 6

Dear Grandchildren,

The date is April 20, 2067, and on this day I have turned eighty years of age. I am not in as good a shape as I used to be, despite modern medicine.

Many times in your youth, you had asked me what life was like when I was ten or eleven or twelve. Every time I have said, "It was like heaven then, even though it was a brutal world." When you asked me why, I would answer, "Some day you will find out." Today is the day you shall find out.

When I was a bit younger than you are, I would dream about the future. Now I dream about the past. Now, even at my old age, I can't even walk into a building without being given the third degree. Police officers might ask me to look through my purse. Of course, I have never said no because of the fear of going to jail. I happen to know that the schools have tight rules and that a stranger can't come in unless the computer has a fingerprint of the person. I will admit that crime has had a drastic decrease. However, I find it annoying. When I was ten, my mother would walk into my school and take me wherever we were going. If she picked me up early she would have to get a permission slip to say why I had left. Now no one can do that.

There are many other reasons. I used to live on a farm and send my cattle to market to be shipped around the nation. Unfortunately only a few farms exist in the United States and everyone eats artificial meat and produce. I believe that the last piece of real meat that I had was when I was seventy-two.

I'm going to end my letter here. Please carry my words with you forever. One of these days, medicine will no longer be able to keep me alive, and I shall leave you forever. I am giving you this letter now and leaving it up to you to be the promise of the new millennium. I will always love you.

Grangran

Dear Grandkids

Sarah Sutton — Homer Pittard Campus School, Grade 6

Dear Grandkids,

Hello, I hope you all are doing well. It is rare for you to receive a letter from me, but this is not an ordinary letter. This is a letter of my concern for the well-being of Earth and its inhabitants and a message to you.

Sixty-eight years ago, when I was about twelve, life was much different than it is now. Although it was not a dream world, it was still much different. We had just begun to realize what trouble our technological advances were causing our earth. The ozone had just begun to deteriorate; we had just begun to realize the effects of nuclear war and deforestation. Many stands were taken at the turn of the century, but not much was done. The global warming we are so aware of now was only just beginning. Prices were lower then, since our natural resources were more abundant. Then, we had only just sent a probe to Mars, and now we are preparing to colonize our moon, and terra-forming Mars for our use in the future. No, then things were complex, yet simple. An oxymoron, but only when compared to what we experience today. I have never been one to worry; my seemingly insubordinate childhood was one I hoped you children could experience. The freedom, independence, and order that we all unconsciously followed out while performing our innocent mischief, you will never be able to experience. In the harsh time we reside in now, you have never known what I did, never truly had to rely on your family, as you all were brought up to be independent and predominantly responsible from youth.

You do not play as we used to play. There are not many trees left for you to climb, streams to wade through, fields to indulge your sports. Only the technology for the day, subtly forced upon you in hopes for a better society.

I plead to you, my children, to help fight for the cause of our earth and people. If only we had put a restraint on how we used our resources eighty years ago, when we still had the chance. Human beings should not be a disease, moving from place to place, but we should instead work for our well-being as well as our planet's. Encourage those around to help, also. Whatever we have left to save on this earth, we must attempt to save.

Grandma

Racial slurs thrown about.

People's lives tossed out.

Waves of new diseases spread.

This is our new millennium?

Chris Young — Oakland High School, Grade 9

Remember to be yourself; that is the most important thing to do. I spent eighty years being someone else. You might be popular by being someone else, but in your heart you will come to find out that people will like you for just you. Stay in school. You won't become anything if you don't. Another thing — drugs — DON'T DO THEM! They are nothing but trouble.

Hope Duke — Thurman Francis School, Grade 6

Dearest Granddaughter

Amy Amonett — Central Middle School, Grade 8

Dearest Granddaughter,

As I look through my window
I see my days ending
as yours are just beginning.
I remember everything
all because you told me
and everything from heaven I will see.
Like your first day of kindergarten
with your muddy shirt
saying you were playing in the dirt.
Or the time you tried out for softball
and didn't make the cut.
Or your first boyfriend,
date and kiss.
Or in the ninth grade
when you made straight A's.
Now you are off to college
deciding what you want to be
will be a challenge.
Doctor, lawyer, nurse, teacher
not quite sure.
Whatever you decide
you have my vote.
You are my granddaughter
and I'll love you for that.

With love always,
Grandma

Dear Grandchildren

Kelsey Stroop — Homer Pittard Campus School, Grade 6

Dear Grandchildren,

I would like to inform you about what the world was like when I was young with the promise of the new millennium. Read very closely, because I want you to understand how lucky you are and how much the human race has accomplished in the past eighty years.

When I was a little girl, we went to school every day except for Saturday and Sunday. We mostly learned out of books, but we did use computers. Our computers were quite primitive compared to the ones you use today. We also drove cars on the ground, not in the air. Flying cars were invented during my time, but they cost one million dollars, which was a lot back then. Cars also ran on gas, not solar power. Our music was different, too. It was not as techno as it is now. Our compact discs were bigger and we had little cassette tapes, too. The only people who ate freeze-dried food were astronauts. We didn't eat pills for our meals either.

I just want you to learn and be proud of your history and never ever forget it. History can repeat itself, but it won't if you learn about it. Take care of the earth and don't let life slip through your fingers. Experience everything that you can and never let anyone tell you that you can't do something. You are the future and you should be proud of it. This is the promise of the new millennium.

Love,
Grand Kels

The Promise of a New Millennium

Austin Clark — Central Middle School, Grade 7

The promise, the promise,
What did it mean to us?
From the threat of Y2K,
To our deliverance from fear,
We left the past behind.
We said, "We will not be blind."
Leave the past and learn from our mistakes.
Our goal will be to prevail.
We will shape our destiny!
Move on but do not forget
Columbine, Waco, and little Elian.
Stand up for the truth and what is right,
And do not let anyone take you from the fight.
That is the promise that lets you sleep at night!

YOU, MY CHILD, WILL GO THROUGH MANY THINGS THAT YOU MAY NOT AGREE WITH BUT JUST KEEP ON PRAYING, AND THE LORD WILL GUIDE YOU THROUGH ALL YOUR TOUGH AND PAINFUL ROADS.

TANGELIA CANNON — THURMAN FRANCIS SCHOOL, GRADE 6

THERE IS ALWAYS THE PROMISE OF A NEW DAY, AND THE CHANCE TO DO SOMETHING THAT WILL CHANGE THE WORLD.

MEGAN JAYNE — SMYRNA MIDDLE SCHOOL, GRADE 8

The Promise of a New Millennium

Christie Schafer — Riverdale High School, Grade 9

The promise of a new millennium that is what I say to you
we gave it our all
we've gone through it all
to make it a better place for you
there has been much to happen
a female president, bio-warfare, and a cruise ship to Mars
we have gone through it all
we gave it our all
to make it a better place for you
for here turns another millennium
where the grass is greener and the air is a little bit cleaner
we went through it all
we've done it all
to make it a better place for you.

Generation M

Geraldine Reneé Johnson — Central Middle School, Grade 8

I am eighty years old
And everyone should be told
About my generation's accomplishments
That could only have been God-sent.

Where do I start with a nickel or dime?
Going and going back into time.

I guess I'll start with music
From rock to pop
We were a jammin' generation
That couldn't be stopped.
Transportation was in heaping mounds
A car, a boat, a train, and a bus
They all have to touch water or ground
Which would you choose if you were us?

The brand styles:
Fubu, Karl Kani, and Calvin Klein
Adidas, Old Navy, and Nike
Cuz everyone wanna be like Mikey.

We invented CD players for CDs
Computers for PC's.

We've made clothes and rings for the toes,
Shoes and rings for the nose,
Rings for the tongue and hairbows,
Rings for the ear as soft as a rose.

There are so many things we
Have accomplished together,
Not you but them and me.
There's no other generation I'd rather be.

In my day and age
Life is just a turning page.
You have to keep up
So every second take a sip out of your cup.

Our world is getting better

It's not near as bad

But there's still no excuse

For the problems that we've had.

Jinan Hassan — Roy Waldron School, Grade 7

The radio, television, and computer all fall into the same category. They basically give us information. Sometimes we use them for fun stuff more than for information. Although some people may think that they're having fun, they're really getting information at the same time. Sometimes getting information can be fun,

John Parrett — Riverdale High School, Grade 11

Technology

Amelia Bennett — Oakland High School, Grade 9

Hovercrafts, electric cars
Moon colonies and trips to Mars
Holograms and 3D TV
A world run by technology.

Pills that make us live much longer
Pills that make the weak much stronger
Cures for all the fatal diseases
Economic growth and trade increases.

This new millennium is promising
A bright future for you and me
Let's make it the best that it can be
With a little help from technology.

If a world could change,

Wouldn't life be perfect?

But life can never be perfect...

Because can a world really change?

Heather Ruse — Oakland High School, Grade 9

...My hope for the new millennium is awareness — or at least kindness. The Promise of a New Millennium? I just have hope. I can't promise anything.

Jenn Hall — Oakland High School, Grade 9

The Promise of the New Millennium
Pema Richeson — Oakland High School, Grade 9

Mankind

Integrity and

Laughter,

Love for fellow man with

Equal rights for all...

Nations joined by peace.

New discoveries bring

Interdependence and

Unity with all

Mankind.

YOU ONLY HAVE ONE CHANCE AT LIFE SO TRY YOUR BEST TO SUCCEED.

KARAH BOYCE — CENTAL MIDDLE SCHOOL, GRADE 7

Special acknowledgement and thanks to the Rutherford County teachers who made this book possible:

Central Middle School
Amy Grunow
LeAnn Hays
Christy Higgins
Cathy Hyatt
Matt Marlatt
Brenda McFarlin
Caroline Ott

Homer Pittard Campus School
Jeff Duke

Kittrell Elementary School
Darla Hight
Debbie Molloy

Lascassas Elementary School
Karen Stroud

LaVergne High School
Susan Price
Kay Trobaugh

McFadden School
Cindy Evans

Oakland High School
Billie Jean Chrisman
Sandra Eaton
Kitty Gannon
Eileen Haynes
Nancy Levi
Mary Sue Persons

Riverdale High School
Becky Hofstetter
Deanna Nezer
Patrick White

Roy Waldron School
Caren Hughes

Smyrna High School
Sherry Price
Jill Walls
Karen Warren

Smyrna Middle School
Ann Gannon
Lois McGonigal
Jan Wadleigh

Thurman Francis School
Kimberly Faulk
Janelle Gehrke
Betty McClure
Janie Reeder
Julie Wankel

Will there be

A peace of nations

Or another

Multitude of wars?

Jonathan Seymore — Oakland High School, Grade 9

To publish a book for your school or not-for-profit organization that complements your academic and financial goals, please contact

Write Together™ Publishing

4064 Nolensville Road, PMB #342
Nashville, TN 37211

Phone: 615-781-1518
Fax: 520-223-4850

www.writetogether.com
fundraising@writetogether.com

9 781930 142527